SCIFAIKUEST
May 2025

6	A Little Help, Please
10	Editorial
15	The Richard E. Schell Page
16	The Herb Kauderer Page
17	The Rita Melissano Page
18	The Yuliia Vereta Page
19	The John Dromey Page
20	The David C. Kopaska-Merkel Page
21	The Ngo Binh Anh Khoa Page
24	The Guy Belleranti Page
25	The Matthew Wilson Page
26	First Contact Goes Awry by Lisa Timpf
27	Flora Fracas by Denise Noe
28	Scifaiku
37	Tanka
38	Other Minimalist Forms
45	Haibun and Drabbun
52	Article: Everything Uncanny and the Witch's Familiar by Robert E. Porter
57	t.santitoro: my favorite poem

THE STAFF OF SCIFAIKUEST:
TERI SANTITORO, EDITOR

SCIFAIKUEST is published quarterly online and in print. The two editions are different.

Cover art "Golden Girl" by Richard E. Schell
Cover design by Marcia A. Borell

Vol. XXII, No. 4   May 2025
Scifaikuest [ISSN 1558-9730] is published quarterly on the 1st day of February, May, August, and November in the United States of America by Hiraeth Publishing, P.O. Box 1248, Tularosa, NM 88352. Copyright 2025 by Hiraeth Publishing. All rights revert to authors and artists upon publication. Nothing may be reproduced in whole or in part without written permission from the authors and artists. Any similarity between places and persons mentioned in the fiction or semi-fiction and real places or persons living or dead is coincidental. Writers and artists guidelines are available online at https://www.hiraethsffh.com/scifaikuest.
Guidelines are also available upon request from Hiraeth Publishing, P.O. Box 1248, Tularosa, NM, 88352, if request is accompanied by a SASE #10 envelope with a first-class US stamp. Subscriptions: $28 for one year [4 issues], $44 for two years [8 issues]. Single copies $9.00 postage paid in the United States. Subscriptions to Canada: $33 for one year, $51 for two years. Single copies $11.00 postage paid to Canada. U.S. and Canadian subscribers remit in U.S. funds. All other countries inquire about rates.

What???
No subscription to
Scifaikuest??

We can fix that . . .

https://www.hiraethsffh.com/product-page/scifaikuest-1

Or get a sample back issue to check us out!

https://www.hiraethsffh.com/shop-1

And a subscription makes a great gift, for a holiday or any time of the year!

Minimalism:
A Handbook of Minimalist Genre Poetic Forms

This handbook contains articles about how to write various minimalist poetry forms such as scifaiku, senryu, sijo, haibun, empat perkataan, ghazals, cinquain, cherita, rengays, rengu, octains, tanka, threesomes, and many more. Each article is written by an expert in that particular poetry form.

Teri Santitoro, aka sakyu, who assembled this handbook, has been the editor of Scifaikuest since 2003.

https://www.hiraethsffh.com/product-page/minimalism-a-handbook-of-minimalist-genre-poetic-forms

A Little Help, Please

In the world of the small indie press we fight a never-ending battle for attention to our work, as writers and in publishing. Here's an example: big publishers [you know who they are] have gobs of $$$ that they can devote to advertising and marketing. Here at Hiraeth Publishing, our advertising budget consists of the deposits for whatever soda bottles and aluminum cans we can find alongside the highways. Anti-littering laws make our task even more difficult . . . ☺

That's where YOU come in. YOU are our best promoter. YOU are the one who can tell others about us. Just send 'em to our website, tell them about our store. That's all. Just that.

Of course, we don't mind if you talk us up. We're pretty good, you know. We have some award-winning and award-nominated writers and artists, plus other voices well-deserving to be heard [not everyone wins awards, right?] but our publications are read-worthy nevertheless.

That number once again is:
www.hiraethsffh.com

Friend us on Facebook at Hiraeth Publishing

Follow us on Twitter at @HiraethPublish1

SALE!!

There's a sale going on!! It's still going on!!

All the books you can order at 20% off the total! Woot!

Buy 1 book; buy 100 books! It's all the same discount. Use the code **BOOKS2025** when you check out.

Go to the Shop at www.hiraethsffh.com and make those selections now!

You'll be glad you did. So will we.

Aliens, Magic, and Monsters
By Lauren McBride

Fun to read. Fun to write. *Aliens, Magic, and Monsters* features poems set in the unlimited and imaginative realm of science fiction, fantasy, and horror. The poems were chosen to showcase over twenty poetic forms from acrostiku to zip, from strict rhyme to free verse, and much more in between. There are guidelines included on how to write each type of poem. Try a sci(na)ku. At only six words, it's sure to interest even the youngest readers.

Type: Juvenile and Young Adult Poetry Manual

Ordering links:
Print: https://www.hiraethsffh.com/product-page/aliens-magic-and-monsters-by-lauren-mcbride

ePub: https://www.hiraethsffh.com/product-page/aliens-magic-and-monsters-by-lauren-mcbride-2

PDF: https://www.hiraethsffh.com/product-page/aliens-magic-and-monsters-by-lauren-mcbride-1

Hello and Happy Spring!

It's been the windiest, most icy winter that I can remember, here in the northeast USA, but I hope that May finds you in warmer, more spring-like climes, and that the Winds of Change bring you happy days, indeed!

In this issue, you will find amazing poetry and artwork dealing with the issues of change. As always, our contributors will delight you with changing times during the recent time-change, when we move toward that period of longer days.

So, sit back and relax in the extended daylight, and enjoy another *Scifaikuest*!

Scifaikuest now has its own ISBN!!! Please inform your local book stores and library that they are now able to ORDER SCIFAIKUEST!!!

You can now find us at Hiraeth Books at:
https://www.hiraethsffh.com/home-1

If you don't have a subscription to our PRINT edition, they are available at:
https://www.hiraethsffh.com/product-page/scifaikuest

And, if you would like to join the select group of contributors by submitting your poetry, artwork or article, you can find our guidelines at: https://www.hiraethsffh.com/scifaikuest

You can also read our ONLINE VERSION at: https://www.hiraethsffh.com/scifaikuest-online

Pssst! Looking for something good to read?

You can get **t.santitoro's** newest book, *The Red Foil,* a SF mystery, at: https://www.hiraethsffh.com/product-page/red-foil-by-t-santitoro

and you can find her novella, *Those Who Die,* at: www.hiraethsffh.com/product-page/those-who-die-by-t-santitoro

You can also order **t.santitoro's** novella, *Adopted Child,* at: https://www.hiraethsffh.com/product-page/adopted-child-by-t-santitoro

And you can still get a copy of her vampire novelette, *The Legend of Trey Valentine,* at: https://www.hiraethsffh.com/product-page/legend-of-trey-valentine-by-teri-santitoro

Let's have a nice, big *Scifaikuest* welcome for our newest contributors: **Umi Agawa, Corinne Hughes, Rita R. Melissano, Ph.D.**

break up season
on Enceladus
our hearts thaw too

-sakyu-

AbracaDrabble
By Tyree Campbell

A drabble is a story containing exactly 100 words. This volume contains drabbles with various science fiction and fantasy themes. In here you'll find trolls, time travel and outer space construction problems, courtesans who take instructions literally, dietary supplements, skip tracers, and demented nursery rhymes, and much more. Some are funny, some poignant, some serious, and some are all three.

Print ($8.00):
https://www.hiraethsffh.com/product-page/abracadrabble-by-tyree-campbell

PDF ($1.29):
https://www.hiraethsffh.com/product-page/abracadrabble-by-tyree-campbell-1

Postcards From Space
By Terrie Leigh Relf

Here are some messages on postcards from space, found aboard a derelict craft that crashed on an arid, lifeless world. The OSPS (Outer Space Postal Service) has delivered these messages to Terrie, who now presents them to you. This is what it is like out there.

https://www.hiraethsffh.com/product-page/postcards-from-space-by-terrie-leigh-relf

Living Bad Dreams
Denise Hatfield

When dreams come alive, there's no telling where they will lead. Everything changes when you realize that, dream or no dream, you're going to die. What do you do then?

Ordering Link:
Print Edition ($9.00):
https://www.hiraethsffh.com/product-page/living-bad-dreams-by-denise-hatfield-1
ePub Edition ($2.99):
https://www.hiraethsffh.com/product-page/living-bad-dreams-by-denise-hatfield-2
PDF Edition ($2.99):
https://www.hiraethsffh.com/product-page/living-bad-dreams-by-denise-hatfield

The Richard E. Schell Page

sharing with friends
unforgettable meal
Mar's first harvest

gorgeous starlit serenity
framed in cockpit's darkness
our last power ceases

three body problem
two suns shine above
how long will this summer last

two lovers halt
alien sunset on shoreline
joined above by paired moons

The Herb Kauderer Page

different times

wall clock displays many
different time zones
including Venus

youthful glee

found in spring cleaning
spare fire extinguisher
a spacewalk joy ride

reconstituted ecosystem

row of pill bottles
wild life waiting for rebirth
you just add water

The Rita Melissano Page

sunflowers
the magnetic fields
of solar flares

a fiery eye
in the hazy Milky Way
black hole

darkness
for two billion years...
frozen moonscapes

The Yuliia Vereta Page

information in
feelings out
no days off

in pixelated dreams
disabilities dissolve
humanity evolves

robobees take flight
whirring wings in neon skies
pollinating code

The John Dromey Page

humans excluded
from using cloning machine
no carbon copies

veteran spacer
zero gravity meister
wizard of aughts

a sham rock in space
the counterfeit meteor
hides little green men

not really psychic
killed by falling cocoanut
while reading a palm

The David C. Kopaska-Merkel Page

we gather
at her grave
coming out party

cat lady
dead in front of her TV
pussy's last meal

full moon
dinner invitation
just bring yourselves

fangs poke through
the wrapping paper
you shouldn't have

The Ngo Binh Anh Khoa Page

head in the Cloud
my brain overloaded with
downloaded files

sudden blackout
commuters in teleporters
remain atomized

witching hour
my pet cat's shadow becomes
humanoid

sleep paralysis
the silhouette of something
crawling toward my bed

Cats and Dogs in Space
Lisa Timpf

Cats in lab coats, running experiments on *us*. Robot dogs roaming Mars. Space-faring canines who mistake alien vessels for fetch toys. There are just some of the images you'll find in here. With inspiration from myths, news stories, nursery rhymes, personal experience, and a lifelong interest in science fiction, the poems are written in a variety of styles for your reading enjoyment. Reaching from the distant past to the far future, and points in between, *Cats and Dogs in Space* invites you to have some fun re-imagining man's best friend—and whatever it is that cats call themselves.

When we beamed the book to the future, here's what readers had to say:
"Purrfectly delightful! Enjoyable for readers of any stripe. Some of these poems are enough to make a cat laugh!" *Festus, ship's cat aboard the Silver Starr Spaceliner Frederika.*

"Meaty as a prime rib bone, and just as much fun to chew on! I'd give it two thumbs up—if I had opposable thumbs . . . " *Pepper, K-9 Operative, Galactic Space Services*

So there you have it! Get *your* claws on a copy today!

Print: www.hiraethsffh.com/product-page/cats-and-dogs-in-space-by-lisa-timpf

ePub: www.hiraethsffh.com/product-page/cats-and-dogs-in-space-by-lisa-timpf-2

The Guy Belleranti Page

all talk no work
I confiscate my droid's phone
too many robot calls

droids dropping like flies
only one possible cause
robotulism

invaders from space
I cannot watch anymore
they've taken my eyes

The Matthew Wilson Page

"Comic Con Season"

six armed alien
walking without suspicion
loving comic con

"The Lazy Babysitter"

children playing tag
too much work
remove their batteries

"No mirrors please"

trip to dentist
the nervous doctor
removing her baby fangs

First Contact Goes Awry
Lisa Timpf

Flora Fracas
Denise Noe

SCIFAIKU

Ice-girl

her thought freezes lakes
her kiss melts my heart
ice never felt so warm

    John Newmark

Apology

tachyon beams
caused temporal disruption
response delayed

    John Newmark

revealing her tentacles
under the dress
summer breeze

    Umi Agawa

failed youth serum trials
accidents will happen
baby steps

    Aurelio Rico Lopez III

interior design
plans for a Martian motel
anything but red

    Randall Andrews

earth shimmers above
lights on in the habitat
astronaut sunset

    Greer Woodward

escape hatch
a covey of quail
fly into the sun

    Rick Jackofsky

Sun Ra—
intergalactic
Egyptian jazz

    Rick Jackofsky

stuck in the past—
she sits beside holograms
of all her exes

    Lisa Timpf
    (see Page 22)

moon colony
my pug and I explore
the renovated dog park

    John J. Dunphy

Planet Palestine

pomegranate seeds bleed
erase the homeland mirage
are there walls in space

    Corinne Hughes

hands that are not hands
revolting graveyard of time
wartime medic tent

    Tony Daly

Faerie Propaganda

on an Irish moor
tales of mist that's formed a door
a child's cry within

    Silvatiicus Riddle

deadly solar flare
status of station personnel--
unknown

    T.R. Jones

High Flying Bird

barn owl's feathers
becoming sprinkled with star dust
flying too high

    G. O. Clark

the time traveler's
first journey—
butterflies

    Greg Schwartz

SENRYU

a knights picnic
dragon fire
burnt marshmallows

    Brian Rosenberger

time travel
I realize mom lies
about her age

    Umi Agawa

disturbingly
my daughter calls my name
to the android nanny

    Laverne Oller and Richard E Schell

child in the mirror
failing to mirror real child
glitch in the matrix

    DJ Tyrer

skeleton
found in shallow grave
wearing my watch

    DJ Tyrer

interstellar spacestation
ever expanding lost & found
eclectic collection

    Lauren McBride

feathered frogs and more
writing New Earth's
first field guide

    Lauren McBride

HORRORKU

to ward off evil
another sigil drawn
with a virgin's blood

    Deborah Karl-Brandt

bruising soft skin
unbreakable the grip of
bone-white fingers

    Deborah Karl-Brandt

last remaining evidence
carefully eliminated
with forethought and lye

    Richard E Schell

poisoned gold sprinkles
on the Oscar Party cake
stars falling

    Greer Woodward

vampire hosts banquet
by invite only
one-way sleepover

    Gary Davis

whizzing past black hole
telepath hears screams
billion lost souls

    Gary Davis

a hasty scrawl in
the Grim Reaper's handwriting
don't resuscitate

    John H. Dromey

Greed

marked with greed
and paternal love
devouring his children

    Benjamin Whitney Norris

Femur

runes carved on the femur
recording
his death's throws

    Benjamin Whitney Norris

lightning-lit undead
our car creeps through hungry hordes
exhaust masking our scent

    Greg Fewer

silver threads of moonlight
tangled creek bed grasses
another broken body obscured

    Julie Allyn Johnson

she weds herself to the night
vows of darkness
her ravenous paramour

    Julie Allyn Johnson

baptismal font
the priest
yanked under

    Greg Schwartz

TANKA

the sixth model
Herb Kauderer

another update
fifth edition colonists
now deemed obsolete
the three-dee printer works on
issuing improved humans

mercury vapor siren
the eerie glow
mercilessly lures
the saturniides
into perpetual orbit

    Rick Jackofsky

amidst ancient ruins
devoid of previous inhabitants
androids waiting
patiently
for their next command

    Richard E Schell

long mining contract
far in the asteroid belt
losing a fortune
half to gambling and liquor
wasting the rest

   Richard E Schell and Laverne Oller

OTHER FORMS

MINIMAL POEM

mother galactica's jack
Denise Noe

jack nimble, jack quick
jack flamed to life
from a candlestick

FIBONACCI

Travelers
Denise Noe

Space
Ship
Flying
Galaxy
Boldly Traveling
On Our Scientific Mission
Learning, Recording, the Secrets of Our
   Milky Way

Scavenger Trip
we
searched
for gas
in fire-wracked
suburbs full of the
undead, but the gas station had
burned, leaving nothing,
and now the
car's out
of
fuel

Greg Fewer

On Encountering Time Travelers at a Bank Robbery
Bright
gold,
This sphere -
warm to touch.
I wanted the cash,
but ladies wearing blue silver
stepped from the vault, valaise dripping with
    my hard labors.
Vanished, dropping this small recompense and
    nothing else.
Now in my pocket, a button
pressed - a rush of light,
a red sky,
two moons.
Why
Me?

Gordon Clark

KIMO

working conditions
Herb Kauderer

water shields block killing radiation
astronauts accept the cost,
dream of naked sunshine

CINQUAIN

I shift
multiple plumes
cybernetic sunset
dyeing a planet's signature
to change

Colleen Anderson

GOGYOHKA

abandoned alien outpost
doors
the only clue
to the builders'
size and shape

(Inspired by the movie Forbidden Planet.)
Lauren McBride

among those odd
non-plant people
father
seems to mean
spore-spreader

Lauren McBride

JOINED POEMS

JOINED FIBONACCI

lost objectivity
Herb Kauderer

all
of
human
history
stored in his hard drive
the monitor passes judgment
once
all
traces
of mankind
are erased from the
Milky Way, he sets course for the
next
world
risking
destruction
from nexus beings
throughout the journey he wishes
he
could

erase
the humans
from his jellyware
as easily as from hard drive
so
that
he can
approach his job
unhaunted, and unaudited
by
the
beings
who crafted
him as guardian
against upstart evolutions

I
had
never
felt so cold
and rapidly rose
frightening
all of
those
who
had come
to see me
this one final time
before my
casket
was
closed

       Guy Belleranti

I
live
in a
haunted house
and always enjoy
when visitors get so frightened
they run out the door
screaming in
terror
which
draws
in more
very brave
souls who soon also
take flight from the house with great fright
which convinces me
that I am
the world's
best
ghost

    Guy Belleranti

        JOINED SCIFAIKU

    The Pigman Suite

    experimental blooms
    transmutations bizarre
    New porcine fauna

    human Hogzilla
    no cage holds his budding rage
    super predator

rock steady bebop
porky pig gone feral
and hunting humans

this porky pig slays
rooting through your guts
never gives an oink

finger bone toothpicks
newly blooming ribcage
taken for his crown

grand liberator
comes to every confinement
piglet rampage

confinement wrecker
loose hog apostles spreading
religion flowers

rumors of sightings
The Story County Pigman
haunted Iowa

golf greens and corn fields
lake shores and small town alleys
hog haunted nightmares

dogs refuse to track
hunters strewn across clearings
not suitable prey

farmers and hunters
learning the deadly lesson
leave Pigman alone

   Joshua E. Borgmann

DRABBUN: *STIR CRAZY* by Debby Feo

When I signed up to be a Colonist on the journey to the Asteroid Sedna241, I was full of "Pioneer Spirit". We would arrive at the asteroid within my lifetime. I would actually get to walk on its surface, in a few decades. Our ship The Explorer17 was not a generational ship, where generations would live and die before their destination was reached.

However, it turned out that even a few decades was too long of a time to be stuck within a spaceship, at least for me.

> Ready to walk out
> Cabin fever has won out
> End to endlessness

HAIBUN: *YOU'VE GOT TO BE KIDDING*
Debby Feo

Be a hero. Discover new horizons. Have your name go down in history. Get a whole bunch of credits put into your bank account, upon your return.

I was assured that the scientists believed that the trip would not be dangerous, as the event horizon of the supermassive black hole was well defined, and that I would just be exploring the very edge. At worst, I might feel a little queasy, as I approached the black hole. My spacesuit would protect me from its radiation.

I'm so over this
This black hole's not what they thought
Stretched to the limit

DRABBUN: *DISAPPEARED* by Debby Feo

"What are you studying?"
Mary looks up at the speaker, a tall, elegant man. "I am doing research on indigenous Martians."
"Quite interesting. What have you discovered?"
"They were much more advanced than Earthlings, particularly in genetics."
"Yes, we are."
"We?"
"Did I say 'we'? I meant that my research agrees with yours."
"How long have you been on Mars?"
"My whole life, with short visits to Earth. I find the increased gravitational pull tiring."
"So, your parents were original Colonists?"
"Not quite. My name is Rupert, and your name?"
"Mary"

together they leave
as the library closes
missing colonist

DRABBUN: *Tramp On A Train*
Denise Noe

Tramp on a train rides a whistle to anywhere. Running his fingers leisurely through his long wavy hair, he takes another swig of hot damn! which does its job, making him more fuzzy wuzzy as he notices the guy sleeping at a corner. Approaching to share his drink or maybe cop a smoke, greets, "Hey guy, how are you?" and nudges his fellow rider whose neck falls easily too-far back, exposing a deep gouge in his red-hollowed throat and the tramp gasps in shock, then sighs.

> another swig of hot damn!
> sitting next to a dead
> tramp on a train

DRABBUN: *You Breathed Your Life Into Me*
Denise Noe

You breathed your life into me when you carved me so carefully and so lovingly from limestone creating me in your image as you carved a head for me and carved my shoulders and my breasts hanging pendulously down to my belly round like your own belly from bearing children and then carving my thick curvy legs and big round butt cheeks and you carved me into being without breathing for tens of thousands of years only to be perched on a tiny pedestal behind glass in this case where the museum curator gazes

    at me
    her most
    superb exhibit

***

DRABBUN: *Too Late*
Tom Guldin

Deciphering the plaque on the overlook — "We cleared the trees for farmland, we needed more to feed the growing mouths. It worked, for awhile, then the land gave out. We moved on and cleared some more, until again the soil gave out and we had to move on. Finally we ran out of places to move on and looked back on what we had left — a wasteland that could no longer support us or our growing mouths, a barren, dusty waterless world. Too late, we realized our folly."

    strange glyphs worn with time
    from long forgotten people,
    barren Martian plane

DRABBUN: *Uncommon Grounds*
Randall Andrews

"I hear they serve stiff drinks here," says the stranger as he slides onto the next barstool.

"That's true," I respond, "but the food sucks."

Having recited our code, we get straight to

business. I set a bullet indiscreetly on the bar.

"Don't worry," I say, "nobody cares about munitions smuggling around here."

Then, more furtively, I unscrew the slug from the casing—which should be filled with explosive powder.

"Smell it," I suggest.

The stranger does and then sighs in delight.

"And it's real?" he asks. "Not synthesized?"

"Straight from Earth."

> interstellar smugglers
> caffeinated contraband
> dark roast as lightspeed

HAIBUN: *There Is Nothing Gentle About Us*
John J. Dunphy

"We will not go gentle into that good night." Resistance members revised the title of Dylan Thomas's poem to serve as our oath. We have vowed that, despite the overwhelming odds against us, we will never give up the struggle. The Resistance doesn't fight merely for its own members. We fight for all humanity.

Yes, all of us will eventually be killed in combat. The extraterrestrials who have invaded Earth possess instruments of destruction that make our species' best weapons seem like children's toys. But, though our cause be hopeless, we will fight until the last of us is slain.

To date, no Resistance member has been taken alive by the Enemy. If we're wounded and can't keep pace with our fellow fighters, we detonate a device fastened to our bodies. In a best-case scenario, we take a few of the Enemy with us.

> the shout of "FREEDOM!"
> followed by
> an explosion
> then wails of pain
> not of this Earth

Messages Crossed
Richard E Schell

Virelle,

I have always been honored to serve with you. You excel with kindness, intelligence, and bravery. There was an immediate bond between us, built on shared mutual respect. I sensed early that your interest in me went beyond mere friendship despite coming from different worlds with drastically different cultures and forms. At that time, I felt uncomfortable because I could not reciprocate in my heart with the same emotional gift that you offered me. Time has changed me. I now find myself attracted to you most genuinely. I deeply regret that I did not see and feel then what I do now. With fear, I worry that I may have lost the one opportunity that many never receive. I sincerely hope that fate will not bind us apart.

matters of the heart
some first impressions
command a price

Jonathan,

I know you are aware that my feelings toward you go beyond mere friendship. Your leadership, character, and values iare as highly respected in my culture as they are in yours. I know you understand my civilization is much more heterogeneous in appearance and culture than what you are used to seeing on Earth. I understand that what might come more easily to us in our world, might be insurmountable for a person from yours. I accept that. Still, as we say in our world, "The heart flies high to where our legs can never take us." I respect your decision and will plan to transfer to another assignment with your blessing. I so wish things could be different between us.

unrequited
wise accept
the heart still hopes

ARTICLE

Everyday Uncanny and the Witch's Familiar: Ku's Grasp on Things (1 & 2)
Robert E. Porter

In the clichéd Lovecraftian tale, a glimpse of the truly alien leaves one at the mercy of alienists. That is, people like Dr. Walter Freeman, who made patients docile and complacent by destroying their frontal lobes with icepicks. The Ramones parodied this kind of treatment in their music video for "Psychotherapy." On the surgeon's table, under the scalpel, the patient's forehead opens up. Out bursts a shrunken head at the end of an umbilical stalk, scaring off the whitecoats before withdrawing behind a scab. The patient then goes on to free his fellows from captivity, for all the good it does them. They wander off like heifers high on grass and headed for the expressway, or the next operating theater.

Speaking of theaters...

Ridley Scott's Alien franchise ripped off A.E. van Vogt's Voyage of the Space Beagle, allegedly. Those weird-tailed parasites? Designed by artist H.R. Giger. And in a letter to Giger's agent, James Cameron praised Giger's work -- even as he made excuses for shutting Giger out of his sequel, Aliens.

"Ironically," said Cameron, "it was the production design of *ALIEN*, with its bizarre, psycho-sexual landscape of the subconscious as created by Mr. Giger, that initially attracted me to the project of a sequel. However, having been a production designer myself before becoming a director, I felt I had to put my own unique stamp on the project. Otherwise, it would have had little meaning for me at that point in my career" and he goes on: "Mr. Giger's visual stamp was so powerful and pervasive in *ALIEN* (a major contributor to its success, I believe) that I felt the risk of being overwhelmed by him and his world, if we had brought him into a production where in a sense, he had more reason to be there than I did." (Cameron)

Cameron would have felt alienated if Giger had walked on the set? How apt! By exploiting others' creative material for his own material gain, Cameron himself was a parasite. Like the fleas in a Wookie's beard, or the leeches in a redshirt Trekkie's breeches, or a certain thorax-busting...

But I digress.

Cameron was a production designer... for B-movie "wonder boy" Roger Corman.

"Roger came through one day," said Cameron, "and he kind of threw down a challenge to everyone in the model shop. Actually, he was kind of pissed off. We're so many weeks away from shooting, and no one had even designed the main character ship for Battle Beyond the Stars. The main space ship had a female computer. It was kind of a HAL 9000, but female. He said, 'I want a design in the next two days.' So it sort of became a sort of design contest, and I thought, OK, it's Roger Corman. He does girls-in-bamboo-cages movies. What is he selling? He sells tits! So I designed a kind of Amazon warrior spaceship – basically a spaceship with tits. It was a cool design. Roger came through and he looked at all the designs, and he stopped at mine and he went: 'This is it, this is exactly what I want.' He said, 'What is this?' And I said, 'This is a spaceship with tits.' And he says, 'Yes, that's exactly what it is. You build it.' So suddenly, I was the guy in the model shop that everyone hated." (Nashawaty)

No wonder Giger's "psycho-sexual" aesthetic resonated with Cameron. It synched with his mentor Corman's mode and mores for milking their target audience.

While I was growing up in the 1980s, my peers recommended the movie Alien not as science fiction or horror. "You'll see her tits!" they said. I never did acquire that all-American fetish for nature's baby food dispensers. But the Alien parasite? A nightmare, which stuck in the craw and shat on pop culture, where it has grown and reproduced countless times. What does it mean? Where does it come from? How should we respond?

Hmm...

In every sexist tinsel town, aren't women hams? Actresses scream in labor, flat on their backs, or they go on and on about the horrors of childbirth, preaching anxiety to expectant mothers. Life imitates art; panic leads to unnecessary pain. Then, epidurals, and the inability to push, and the necessity of further intervention. Some butcher in pink scrubs hacking the child out of the womb, for ex. With the increased risk of infection, a longer, more painful recovery, etc. Reinforcing and spreading those anxieties, bringing even more of those horrors to life.

What is the alternative? Babies grown in a Petrie dish? Or should we settle down and quit overcomplicating things? Imagine! Working with, rather than against, anatomy and physiology. Allowing nature to take its course.

What is a fetus, anyway? A parasite growing inside the mother, living off her. Later on, this thing comes out looking like raw sausage in its casing. It will, hopefully, clutch at a milk-engorged breast and suck -- as B-movie horrors do.

That's life!

Of course, every child brought into this world is an alien... and a first contact story. Why should we let them invade? And consume our limited resources? Even take our places, one day? Puppet snatchers! Body masters! As Jack Heinlein and Robert Finney warned us, decades ago. But it was fun making these little monsters, wasn't it? And we have a chance to teach them more than we'll every know. In any case, better to change their diapers than wipe them out... on the walls, the carpet, and the dog. "Arf!"

In ku, we doggedly go for "Aha!" instead. We can often get to that point -- and with more horrific speed and post-human efficiency than I did here -- by looking for the uncanny in the everyday, or the unearthly in the witch's familiar.

WORKS CITED

Cameron, James. "Letter to Leslie Barany," 13 Feb 1987. HR Giger. (https://www.hrgiger.com.) Accessed 13 August 2022.

Nashawaty, Chris. Crab Monsters, Teenage Cavemen, and Candy Stripe Nurses: Roger Corman: King of the B-Movies. Abrams, 2013.

FAVORITE POEM
by editor, t.santitoro

Not to be repetitive, but take another good look at these three awesome poems:

Tramp On A Train
Denise Noe

   Tramp on a train rides a whistle to anywhere. Running his fingers leisurely through his long wavy hair, he takes another swig of hot damn! which does its job, making him more fuzzy wuzzy as he notices the guy sleeping at a corner. Approaching to share his drink or maybe cop a smoke, greets, "Hey guy, how are you?" and nudges his fellow rider whose neck falls easily too-far back, exposing a deep gouge in his red-hollowed throat and the tramp gasps in shock, then sighs.
        another swig of hot damn!
        sitting next to a dead
        tramp on a train

I love it! What an unexpected story! Love how it starts and ends with the same phrase.

OR:

youthful glee
Herb Kauderer

found in spring cleaning
spare fire extinguisher
a spacewalk joy ride

I especially love "Youthful Glee"! What a wonderful picture this poem conjures! Wheeeeeee!!! LOL!! FANTASTIC ah-ha moment and "show don't tell" writing!

OR:

last remaining evidence
carefully eliminated
with forethought and lye

Richard E Schell

WOW! I LOVE this poem!!! This is succinct, concise and POWERFUL! Totally awesome! This says SOOO MUCH, so perfectly!

Okay, Readers, what do YOU think? Do you have a favorite?

www.ingramcontent.com/pod-product-compliance
Lightning Source LLC
LaVergne TN
LVHW021953060526
838201LV00049B/1687